30 — THE BIG THREE-OH

Written By:
Herbert I. Kavet

Illustrated By:
Martin Riskin

© 1991
by **Ivory Tower Publishing Company, Inc.**
All Rights Reserved

30 29 28 27 26 25 24 23 22 21 20 19 18 17 16 15 14 13 12 11 10 9 8 7

Ivory Tower Publishing Co., Inc.

MILTON KNEW HE SHOULD NEVER COUNT ON
HIS PARENTS FOR A BLIND DATE.

MISSY FORGOT TO CHECK TO SEE IF HER BLIND DATE
HAD A CAR.

DOUGLAS FINALLY OWNS A CAR THAT IS TOTALLY PAID FOR.

JENNIE STILL LOVED A TAN BUT WAS STARTING TO WORRY ABOUT THE
LONG-TERM EFFECTS OF THE SUN.

SHEILA PERFECTED ONE EXOTIC RECIPE THAT SHE USES
WHENEVER IMPORTANT COMPANY COMES.

"REMEMBER WHEN WE USED TO CHOOSE A CEREAL FOR THE TOYS IN IT?"
BRAN BOMBS
MOVING CEREAL
FIBRE CRUNCH
PRUNE NUTTERS
FIBRE JACKS

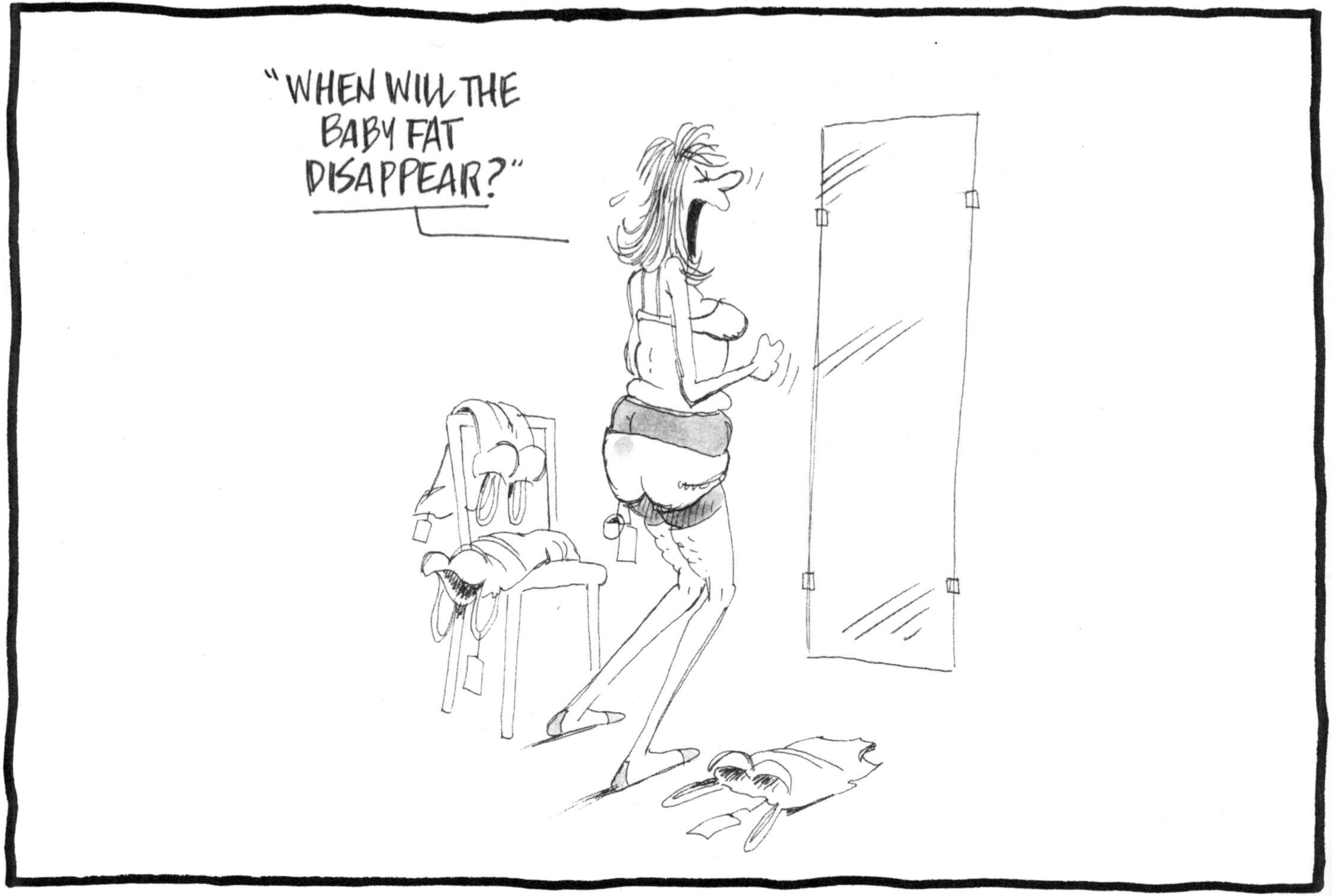
"WHEN WILL THE BABY FAT DISAPPEAR?"

"LET'S SEE IF I HAVE THIS STRAIGHT. I PICK UP PIZZA AFTER DROPPING LISA AT GYMNASTICS AND RETURNING THE MOVIE. I CAN GET A HAIRCUT IF THE CAR INSPECTION TAKES MORE THAN AN HOUR, OTHERWISE CHECK THE SOCCER FIELD FOR JOHN'S HOMEWORK ASSIGNMENT. RETURN THE BURST FERTILIZER BAG AND BUY A WHITE WINE FOR THE SCHUMACHERS.

JACQUELINE IS ALMOST POSITIVE THAT HOROSCOPES
ARE TOTAL BUNK.

"THIS IS YOUR MOTHER, DEAR, REMEMBER ME? I'M SURE YOU'RE VERY BUSY SINCE YOU HAVEN'T PHONED ALL WEEK, BUT PLEASE TRY TO GIVE A QUICK CALL JUST TO LET ME KNOW YOU'RE STILL ALIVE. AUNT SOPHIE IS COMING OVER ON SUNDAY AND WOULD LOVE TO SEE YOU. YOU KNOW HOW SHE ALWAYS REMEMBE
YOUR BIRTHDAY SO TRY REALLY HARD TO MAKE IT."

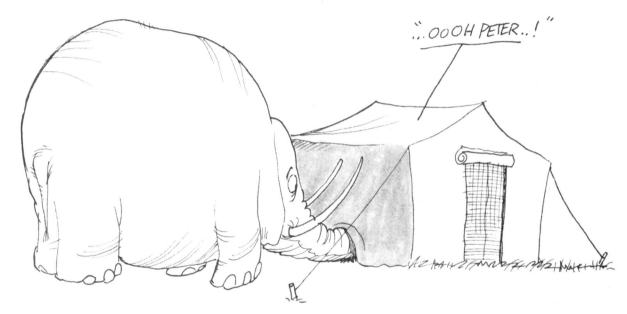

PETER AND FRANCINE FINALLY TAKE THE AFRICAN SAFARI THEY HAVE
BEEN DREAMING ABOUT.

GORMAN REALIZES PAULETTE HAS DISCOVERED A NEW DIET PROGRAM.

NORMAN'S JOB SECURITY RESTED ON THE FACT THAT
HE WAS THE ONLY PERSON WHO COULD PROGRAM THE BOSS'S
TELEPHONE.

WITH THE HELP OF THEIR NEW RADAR DETECTOR, CINDY AND PHIL MAKE IT TO THE BEACH IN RECORD TIME.

ALBERT FINDS HIS CELLULAR PHONE BILL IS BIGGER THAN HIS CAR
PAYMENT THIS MONTH.

CONGRATULATIONS, YOU MAY HAVE POSITIVELY WON $1,000,000.⁰⁰ CASH OR ONE OF THESE OTHER VALUABLE PRIZES.

NOW THAT URSULA IS 30, HER NIECES AND NEPHEWS CAN'T TALK HER INTO ACTIVITIES SHE'D REALLY RATHER NOT DO.

"HER YOUNGER SISTER JUST GOT ENGAGED."

THE HEALTH POLICE ARRIVED JUST AS SAMANTHA AND THERMOND FINISHED THEIR SECOND CUP OF COFFEE IN THE NO SMOKING SECTION.

"MARTY'S COMMITMENT TO HIS VEGETARIAN DIET WEAKENS WHENEVER HE GOES TO A BALL GAME."

ARTHUR LEARNED TO COMPLAIN LOUDLY ABOUT POOR WORKMANSHIP ON HIS CAR.

HORTENSE KNEW ALL THE TRICKS FOR STARTING HER CAR
ON A COLD SNOWY DAY.

VINCENT HAD ENOUGH EXPERIENCES AT 30 SO HE NO
LONGER HAD TO LIE ON HIS RESUME.

SONJA HAS JUST ABOUT GIVEN UP WAITING FOR SOMEONE TO COME OVER WHO WILL OFFER TO TAKE OUT THE GARBAGE.

NOW THAT LESTER TURNED 30, HE FOUND HE WAS TREATED WITH MORE RESPECT AT WORK.

"I THOUGHT YOU PICKED UP MATTHEW."

PATRICIA AND JONATHAN LEARN ABOUT CLOSING
COSTS WHEN BUYING THEIR FIRST HOME.

BLANCH PREPARES A TYPICIAL ANGOLAN MEAL FOR PORTIA AND
RAYMOND THAT SHE LEARNED IN THE PEACE CORPS.

WANTING TO MELT OFF A FEW EXTRA POUNDS, THELMA AND RODERICK GOT TALKED INTO A LIFETIME MEMBERSHIP AT THEIR LOCAL HEALTH CLUB.